BEING
Journaling the Journey

www.mildredblack.com

mildredblack

First edition ISBN: 9798218228873

Advisor: Alexandria Cunningham
Cover art by Latrisha Redmon
Typesetting by Latrisha Redmon

Mildred Black
1601 5th Avenue N
Suite 150
Birmingham, Alabama 35205

mildredblack.com

mildredblack

Citations

The New American Bible. (1992).

Maslow, A. H. (1998). *Toward a psychology of being.* John Wiley & Sons Incorporated.

Batz, P., & Schmidt, T. (2014). *What really works: Blending the 7 f's for the life you imagine.* Bookhouse Fulfillment.

Jenkins, M. (2021). What Do We Need to Stop, Start, or Continue?. In Expert Humans: Critical Leadership Skills for a Disrupted World. Emerald Publishing Limited.

Darbi, W. P. K. (2012). Of mission and vision statements and their potential impact on employee behavior and attitudes: The case of a public but profit-oriented tertiary institution. *International Journal of Business and Social Science,* 3(14).

r.rossington. (2021, September 27). The importance of aligning your personal and professional mission statements. *CEO Today.* https://www.ceotodaymagazine.com/2021/09/the-importance-of-aligning-your-personal-and-professional-mission-statements/

Solutions, R. (2017, August 22). How to write a personal mission statement. *Ramsey Solutions.* https://www.ramseysolutions.com/personal-growth/mission-statement-101

Herrity, J. (2019, October 7). A step-by-step guide to creating a personal vision statement. *Indeed Career Guide.* https://www.indeed.com/career-advice/career-development/personal-vision-statement

This journal belongs to

Welcome to Being, Journaling the Journey!

Being is thriving. In his book, Toward a Psychology of Being, Abraham Maslow deals with the correlation between our mindsets and the level to which our human needs are being met. He describes human needs as being prioritized in a hierarchy. Maslow's Hierarchy of Needs identifies five levels.

The first four — surviving, living, belonging, and accomplishing — serve as the platform on which being can happen. Being is the lifelong movement toward the best version of yourself, reaching toward your full potential. Maslow refers to it as "self-actualizing."

The book that you are holding is a guided journal to support you on your journey toward being. It is designed to empower you to capture your big picture vision and translate it into intentional, daily actions.

There are two major sections to this guided journal:

Section 1:

Big Picture Journaling: *This section will help you to evaluate, clarify and set intentions.*

You will have prompts to guide you to

- evaluate your life
- capture your mission
- cast your vision
- set clear intentions

Section 2:

Daily Journaling: *This section will prompt you to start and end each day with clarity, intention, and power. You will have space to start each day with gratitude, confessions, and intention, and center on your itinerary.*

During the day you will be prompted to do a personal check-in, celebrate your wins, and end each day with forgiveness and reflections.

Thank you for choosing this journal as a tool to be on the journey with you toward BEING!

Are you ready? Let's get started!

Sincerely and truly yours,

Mildred Black

<u>Big Picture Journaling</u>

This section will help you to evaluate, clarify and set intentions.
You will have prompts to guide you to

-evaluate your life
-capture your mission
-cast your vision
-set clear intentions

The Big Picture

Personal Evaluation

Pictured below is Maslow's Hierarchy of Needs.

Please use the spaces below to rate your life at each level
on the hierarchy on a scale of 1-10.

Also, make notes on why you rated each level as you did.

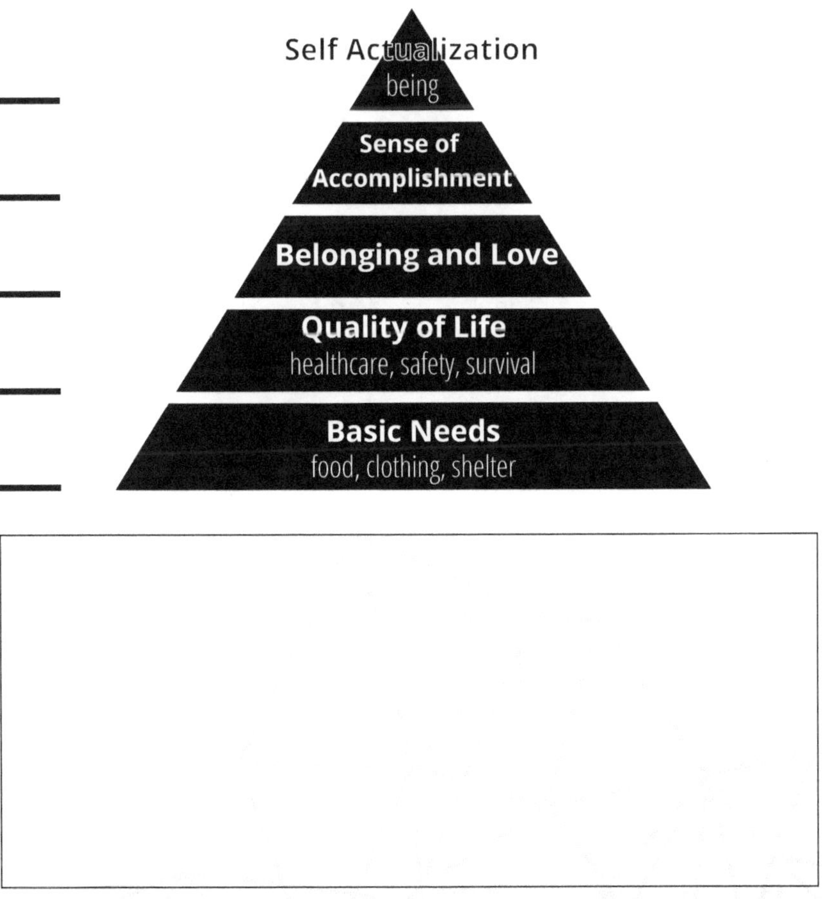

Life Zones

Pictured below is a graph of eight life zones.

Please use the spaces below to rate your life at each level on a scale of 1-10.

Also, make notes on why you rated each level as you did.

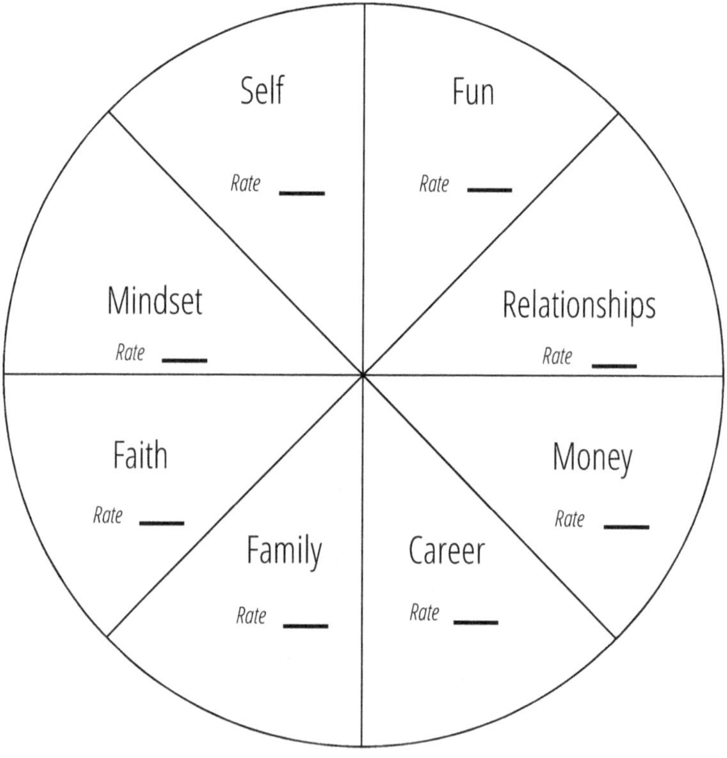

Start/Stop/Continue

Now that you've done this personal evaluation,
what are some things you want to start, stop and continue?

Start	Stop	Continue

My Mission Statement

Your mission statement is that which describes your purpose, your why.

It answers the questions:

- What problem do I solve?
- What is my purpose?

Please be patient with yourself. It takes times to develop a personal mission statement and it may change over time.

Use the space below to write your personal mission statement.

What is your mission statement?

My Vision Statement

Your vision statement describes the ultimate outcome of your mission. It's the picture of what you see as your destination.

Just as with developing your mission statement, be patient with yourself. It takes time to develop a vision statement and it may change over time.

Use the space below to write or draw your vision.

What is your vision statement?

Use the space below to write or draw your outlook in 1 year, 3 years and 5 years.

1 Year Outlook

3 Year Outlook

5 Year Outlook

My Big 3 Intentions

Use the space below to write your big 3 intentions.

01

02

03

2023 Calendar

January

Su	Mo	Tu	We	Th	Fr	Sa
1	2	3	4	5	6	7
8	9	10	11	12	13	14
15	16	17	18	19	20	21
22	23	24	25	26	27	28
29	30	31				

February

Su	Mo	Tu	We	Th	Fr	Sa
			1	2	3	4
5	6	7	8	9	10	11
12	13	14	15	16	17	18
19	20	21	22	23	24	25
26	27	28				

March

Su	Mo	Tu	We	Th	Fr	Sa
			1	2	3	4
5	6	7	8	9	10	11
12	13	14	15	16	17	18
19	20	21	22	23	24	25
26	27	28	29	30	31	

April

Su	Mo	Tu	We	Th	Fr	Sa
						1
2	3	4	5	6	7	8
9	10	11	12	13	14	15
16	17	18	19	20	21	22
23	24	25	26	27	28	29
30						

May

Su	Mo	Tu	We	Th	Fr	Sa
	1	2	3	4	5	6
7	8	9	10	11	12	13
14	15	16	17	18	19	20
21	22	23	24	25	26	27
28	29	30	31			

June

Su	Mo	Tu	We	Th	Fr	Sa
				1	2	3
4	5	6	7	8	9	10
11	12	13	14	15	16	17
18	19	20	21	22	23	24
25	26	27	28	29	30	

July

Su	Mo	Tu	We	Th	Fr	Sa
						1
2	3	4	5	6	7	8
9	10	11	12	13	14	15
16	17	18	19	20	21	22
23	24	25	26	27	28	29
30	31					

August

Su	Mo	Tu	We	Th	Fr	Sa
		1	2	3	4	5
6	7	8	9	10	11	12
13	14	15	16	17	18	19
20	21	22	23	24	25	26
27	28	29	30	31		

September

Su	Mo	Tu	We	Th	Fr	Sa
					1	2
3	4	5	6	7	8	9
10	11	12	13	14	15	16
17	18	19	20	21	22	23
24	25	26	27	28	29	30

October

Su	Mo	Tu	We	Th	Fr	Sa
1	2	3	4	5	6	7
8	9	10	11	12	13	14
15	16	17	18	19	20	21
22	23	24	25	26	27	28
29	30	31				

November

Su	Mo	Tu	We	Th	Fr	Sa
			1	2	3	4
5	6	7	8	9	10	11
12	13	14	15	16	17	18
19	20	21	22	23	24	25
26	27	28	29	30		

December

Su	Mo	Tu	We	Th	Fr	Sa
					1	2
3	4	5	6	7	8	9
10	11	12	13	14	15	16
17	18	19	20	21	22	23
24	25	26	27	28	29	30
31						

2024 Calendar

January

Su	Mo	Tu	We	Th	Fr	Sa
	1	2	3	4	5	6
7	8	9	10	11	12	13
14	15	16	17	18	19	20
21	22	23	24	25	26	27
28	29	30	31			

February

Su	Mo	Tu	We	Th	Fr	Sa
				1	2	3
4	5	6	7	8	9	10
11	12	13	14	15	16	17
18	19	20	21	22	23	24
25	26	27	28	29		

March

Su	Mo	Tu	We	Th	Fr	Sa
					1	2
3	4	5	6	7	8	9
10	11	12	13	14	15	16
17	18	19	20	21	22	23
24	25	26	27	28	29	30
31						

April

Su	Mo	Tu	We	Th	Fr	Sa
	1	2	3	4	5	6
7	8	9	10	11	12	13
14	15	16	17	18	19	20
21	22	23	24	25	26	27
28	29	30				

May

Su	Mo	Tu	We	Th	Fr	Sa
			1	2	3	4
5	6	7	8	9	10	11
12	13	14	15	16	17	18
19	20	21	22	23	24	25
26	27	28	29	30	31	

June

Su	Mo	Tu	We	Th	Fr	Sa
						1
2	3	4	5	6	7	8
9	10	11	12	13	14	15
16	17	18	19	20	21	22
23	24	25	26	27	28	29
30						

Daily Journaling

This section will prompt you to start and end each day with clarity, intention, and power.

You will have space to start each day with gratitude, confessions, and intention, and center on your itinerary.

During the day you will be prompted to do a personal check-in, celebrate your wins, and end each day with forgiveness and reflections.

Jan Feb Mar Apr May Jun Jul Aug Sep Oct Nov Dec

1 2 3 4 5 6 7 8 9 10 11 12 13 14 15 16 17 18 19 20 21 22 23 24 25 26 27 28 29 30 31

Sunday Monday Tuesday Wednesday Thursday Friday Saturday

My Itinerary

6AM	
7AM	
8AM	
9AM	
10AM	
11AM	
12PM	
1PM	
2PM	
3PM	
4PM	
5PM	
6PM	
7PM	
8PM	
9PM	
10PM	

Notes

3 things I'm grateful for

○

○

○

My intentions

○

○

○

○

My priorities

○

○

○

○

Personal Check-in

| How Am I Doing? | What Do I Need? | What Can I Start? |

New Contacts

Name	Phone	Email	Follow Up Note

Celebrate Wins

| People Served | Breakthrough Moments |

To Do Items

Reflections

| What Went Well | Lessons Learned | Apologies I Should Make |

| Who Should I Forgive | Points of Clarity | 3 Things I'm Grateful For |

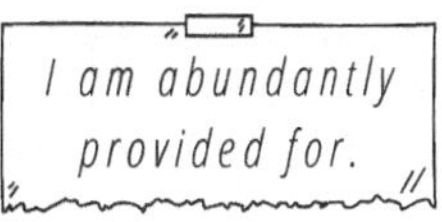

My Itinerary

6AM	
7AM	
8AM	
9AM	
10AM	
11AM	
12PM	
1PM	
2PM	
3PM	
4PM	
5PM	
6PM	
7PM	
8PM	
9PM	
10PM	

Notes

3 things I'm grateful for

My intentions

My priorities

Personal Check-in

How Am I Doing?

What Do I Need?

What Can I Start?

New Contacts

Name	Phone	Email	Follow Up Note

Celebrate Wins

People Served

Breakthrough Moments

To Do Items

Reflections

What Went Well

Lessons Learned

Apologies I Should Make

Who Should I Forgive

Points of Clarity

3 Things I'm Grateful For

Jan   Feb   Mar   Apr   May   Jun   Jul   Aug   Sep   Oct   Nov   Dec
1 2 3 4 5 6 7 8 9 10 11 12 13 14 15 16 17 18 19 20 21 22 23 24 25 26 27 28 29 30 31
Sunday   Monday   Tuesday   Wednesday   Thursday   Friday   Saturday

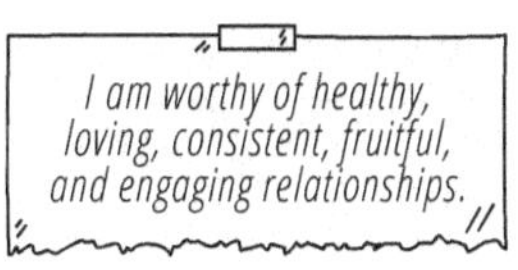

My Itinerary

6AM	
7AM	
8AM	
9AM	
10AM	
11AM	
12PM	
1PM	
2PM	
3PM	
4PM	
5PM	
6PM	
7PM	
8PM	
9PM	
10PM	

Notes

3 things I'm grateful for

- ○
- ○
- ○

My intentions

- ○
- ○
- ○
- ○

My priorities

- ○
- ○
- ○
- ○

Personal Check-in

How Am I Doing?

What Do I Need?

What Can I Start?

New Contacts

Name	Phone	Email	Follow Up Note

Celebrate Wins

People Served	Breakthrough Moments

To Do Items

Reflections

What Went Well

Lessons Learned

Apologies I Should Make

Who Should I Forgive

Points of Clarity

3 Things I'm Grateful For

Jan   Feb   Mar   Apr   May   Jun   Jul   Aug   Sep   Oct   Nov   Dec
1 2 3 4 5 6 7 8 9 10 11 12 13 14 15 16 17 18 19 20 21 22 23 24 25 26 27 28 29 30 31
Sunday   Monday   Tuesday   Wednesday   Thursday   Friday   Saturday

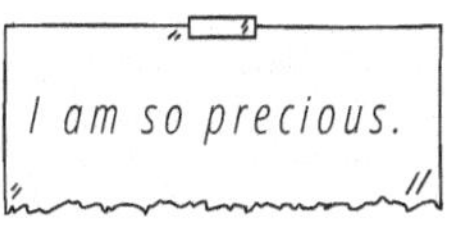

My Itinerary

6AM	
7AM	
8AM	
9AM	
10AM	
11AM	
12PM	
1PM	
2PM	
3PM	
4PM	
5PM	
6PM	
7PM	
8PM	
9PM	
10PM	

Notes

3 things I'm grateful for

○

○

○

My intentions

○

○

○

○

My priorities

○

○

○

○

Personal Check-in

How Am I Doing?	What Do I Need?	What Can I Start?

New Contacts

Name	Phone	Email	Follow Up Note

Celebrate Wins

To Do Items

People Served	Breakthrough Moments

Reflections

What Went Well	Lessons Learned	Apologies I Should Make

Who Should I Forgive	Points of Clarity	3 Things I'm Grateful For

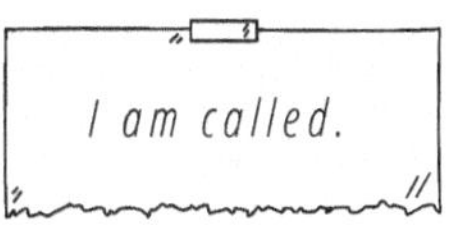

My Itinerary

6AM
7AM
8AM
9AM
10AM
11AM
12PM
1PM
2PM
3PM
4PM
5PM
6PM
7PM
8PM
9PM
10PM

Notes

3 things I'm grateful for

○

○

○

My intentions

○

○

○

○

My priorities

○

○

○

○

Personal Check-in

How Am I Doing?

What Do I Need?

What Can I Start?

New Contacts

Name	Phone	Email	Follow Up Note

Celebrate Wins

People Served	Breakthrough Moments

To Do Items

Reflections

What Went Well

Lessons Learned

Apologies I Should Make

Who Should I Forgive

Points of Clarity

3 Things I'm Grateful For

Jan   Feb   Mar   Apr   May   Jun   Jul   Aug   Sep   Oct   Nov   Dec
1 2 3 4 5 6 7 8 9 10 11 12 13 14 15 16 17 18 19 20 21 22 23 24 25 26 27 28 29 30 31
Sunday   Monday   Tuesday   Wednesday   Thursday   Friday   Saturday

My Itinerary

6AM	
7AM	
8AM	
9AM	
10AM	
11AM	
12PM	
1PM	
2PM	
3PM	
4PM	
5PM	
6PM	
7PM	
8PM	
9PM	
10PM	

Notes

3 things I'm grateful for

○

○

○

My intentions

○

○

○

○

My priorities

○

○

○

○

Personal Check-in

How Am I Doing?	What Do I Need?	What Can I Start?

New Contacts

Name	Phone	Email	Follow Up Note

Celebrate Wins

People Served	Breakthrough Moments

To Do Items

Reflections

What Went Well	Lessons Learned	Apologies I Should Make

Who Should I Forgive	Points of Clarity	3 Things I'm Grateful For

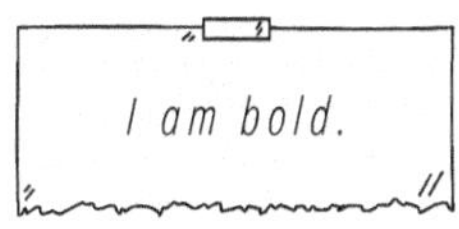

My Itinerary

6AM	
7AM	
8AM	
9AM	
10AM	
11AM	
12PM	
1PM	
2PM	
3PM	
4PM	
5PM	
6PM	
7PM	
8PM	
9PM	
10PM	

Notes

3 things I'm grateful for

○

○

○

My intentions

○

○

○

○

My priorities

○

○

○

○

Personal Check-in

How Am I Doing?	What Do I Need?	What Can I Start?

New Contacts

Name	Phone	Email	Follow Up Note

Celebrate Wins

People Served	Breakthrough Moments

To Do Items

Reflections

What Went Well	Lessons Learned	Apologies I Should Make

Who Should I Forgive	Points of Clarity	3 Things I'm Grateful For

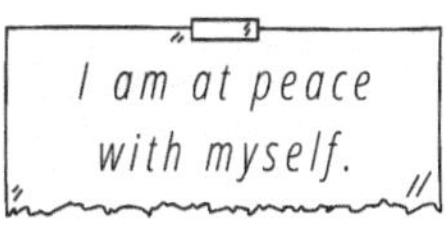

My Itinerary

6AM	
7AM	
8AM	
9AM	
10AM	
11AM	
12PM	
1PM	
2PM	
3PM	
4PM	
5PM	
6PM	
7PM	
8PM	
9PM	
10PM	

Notes

3 things I'm grateful for

My intentions

My priorities

Personal Check-in

How Am I Doing?

What Do I Need?

What Can I Start?

New Contacts

Name	Phone	Email	Follow Up Note

Celebrate Wins

People Served

Breakthrough Moments

To Do Items

Reflections

What Went Well

Lessons Learned

Apologies I Should Make

Who Should I Forgive

Points of Clarity

3 Things I'm Grateful For

Jan   Feb   Mar   Apr   May   Jun   Jul   Aug   Sep   Oct   Nov   Dec
1 2 3 4 5 6 7 8 9 10 11 12 13 14 15 16 17 18 19 20 21 22 23 24 25 26 27 28 29 30 31
Sunday   Monday   Tuesday   Wednesday   Thursday   Friday   Saturday

My Itinerary

6AM	
7AM	
8AM	
9AM	
10AM	
11AM	
12PM	
1PM	
2PM	
3PM	
4PM	
5PM	
6PM	
7PM	
8PM	
9PM	
10PM	

Notes

3 things I'm grateful for

- ○
- ○
- ○

My intentions

- ○
- ○
- ○
- ○

My priorities

- ○
- ○
- ○
- ○

Personal Check-in

How Am I Doing?

What Do I Need?

What Can I Start?

New Contacts

Name	Phone	Email	Follow Up Note

Celebrate Wins

People Served

Breakthrough Moments

To Do Items

Reflections

What Went Well

Lessons Learned

Apologies I Should Make

Who Should I Forgive

Points of Clarity

3 Things I'm Grateful For

Jan   Feb   Mar   Apr   May   Jun   Jul   Aug   Sep   Oct   Nov   Dec

1 2 3 4 5 6 7 8 9 10 11 12 13 14 15 16 17 18 19 20 21 22 23 24 25 26 27 28 29 30 31

Sunday   Monday   Tuesday   Wednesday   Thursday   Friday   Saturday

My Itinerary

6AM	
7AM	
8AM	
9AM	
10AM	
11AM	
12PM	
1PM	
2PM	
3PM	
4PM	
5PM	
6PM	
7PM	
8PM	
9PM	
10PM	

Notes

3 things I'm grateful for

○

○

○

My intentions

○

○

○

○

My priorities

○

○

○

○

Personal Check-in

How Am I Doing?	What Do I Need?	What Can I Start?

New Contacts

Name	Phone	Email	Follow Up Note

Celebrate Wins

People Served	Breakthrough Moments

To Do Items

Reflections

What Went Well	Lessons Learned	Apologies I Should Make

Who Should I Forgive	Points of Clarity	3 Things I'm Grateful For

Jan Feb Mar Apr May Jun Jul Aug Sep Oct Nov Dec
1 2 3 4 5 6 7 8 9 10 11 12 13 14 15 16 17 18 19 20 21 22 23 24 25 26 27 28 29 30 31
Sunday Monday Tuesday Wednesday Thursday Friday Saturday

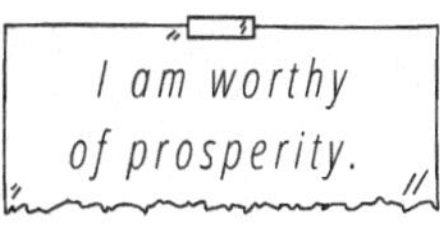

My Itinerary

6 AM	
7 AM	
8 AM	
9 AM	
10 AM	
11 AM	
12 PM	
1 PM	
2 PM	
3 PM	
4 PM	
5 PM	
6 PM	
7 PM	
8 PM	
9 PM	
10 PM	

Notes

3 things I'm grateful for

○

○

○

My intentions

○

○

○

○

My priorities

○

○

○

○

Personal Check-in

How Am I Doing?	What Do I Need?	What Can I Start?

New Contacts

Name	Phone	Email	Follow Up Note

Celebrate Wins

People Served	Breakthrough Moments

To Do Items

Reflections

What Went Well	Lessons Learned	Apologies I Should Make

Who Should I Forgive	Points of Clarity	3 Things I'm Grateful For

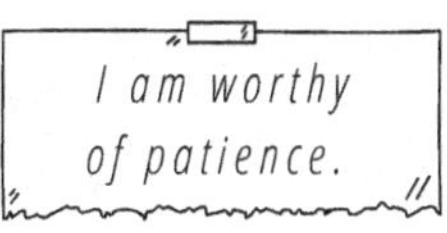

My Itinerary

Time	
6 AM	
7 AM	
8 AM	
9 AM	
10 AM	
11 AM	
12 PM	
1 PM	
2 PM	
3 PM	
4 PM	
5 PM	
6 PM	
7 PM	
8 PM	
9 PM	
10 PM	

Notes

3 things I'm grateful for

- ○
- ○
- ○

My intentions

- ○
- ○
- ○
- ○

My priorities

- ○
- ○
- ○
- ○

Personal Check-in

How Am I Doing?

What Do I Need?

What Can I Start?

New Contacts

Name	Phone	Email	Follow Up Note

Celebrate Wins

People Served

Breakthrough Moments

To Do Items

Reflections

What Went Well

Lessons Learned

Apologies I Should Make

Who Should I Forgive

Points of Clarity

3 Things I'm Grateful For

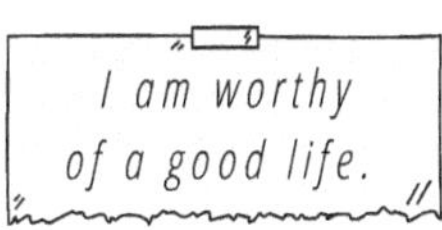

My Itinerary

6AM	
7AM	
8AM	
9AM	
10AM	
11AM	
12PM	
1PM	
2PM	
3PM	
4PM	
5PM	
6PM	
7PM	
8PM	
9PM	
10PM	

Notes

3 things I'm grateful for

○

○

○

My intentions

○

○

○

○

My priorities

○

○

○

○

Personal Check-in

How Am I Doing?	What Do I Need?	What Can I Start?

New Contacts

Name	Phone	Email	Follow Up Note

Celebrate Wins

To Do Items

People Served	Breakthrough Moments

Reflections

What Went Well	Lessons Learned	Apologies I Should Make

Who Should I Forgive	Points of Clarity	3 Things I'm Grateful For

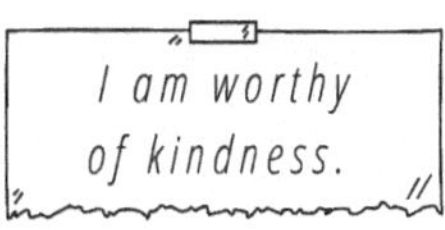

My Itinerary

6AM	
7AM	
8AM	
9AM	
10AM	
11AM	
12PM	
1PM	
2PM	
3PM	
4PM	
5PM	
6PM	
7PM	
8PM	
9PM	
10PM	

Notes

3 things I'm grateful for

My intentions

My priorities

How Am I Doing?   What Do I Need?   What Can I Start?

New Contacts

Name	Phone	Email	Follow Up Note

Celebrate Wins

People Served   Breakthrough Moments

To Do Items

Reflections

What Went Well   Lessons Learned   Apologies I Should Make

Who Should I Forgive   Points of Clarity   3 Things I'm Grateful For

Jan   Feb   Mar   Apr   May   Jun   Jul   Aug   Sep   Oct   Nov   Dec
1 2 3 4 5 6 7 8 9 10 11 12 13 14 15 16 17 18 19 20 21 22 23 24 25 26 27 28 29 30 31
Sunday   Monday   Tuesday   Wednesday   Thursday   Friday   Saturday

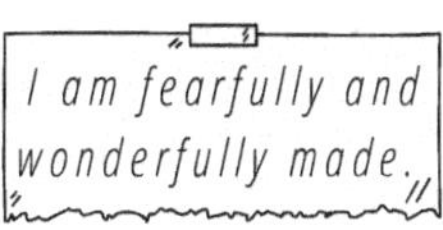

My Itinerary

6AM	
7AM	
8AM	
9AM	
10AM	
11AM	
12PM	
1PM	
2PM	
3PM	
4PM	
5PM	
6PM	
7PM	
8PM	
9PM	
10PM	

3 things I'm grateful for

My intentions

My priorities

Notes

Personal Check-in

How Am I Doing?	What Do I Need?	What Can I Start?

New Contacts

Name	Phone	Email	Follow Up Note

Celebrate Wins

People Served	Breakthrough Moments

To Do Items

Reflections

What Went Well	Lessons Learned	Apologies I Should Make

Who Should I Forgive	Points of Clarity	3 Things I'm Grateful For

Jan Feb Mar Apr May Jun Jul Aug Sep Oct Nov Dec
1 2 3 4 5 6 7 8 9 10 11 12 13 14 15 16 17 18 19 20 21 22 23 24 25 26 27 28 29 30 31
Sunday Monday Tuesday Wednesday Thursday Friday Saturday

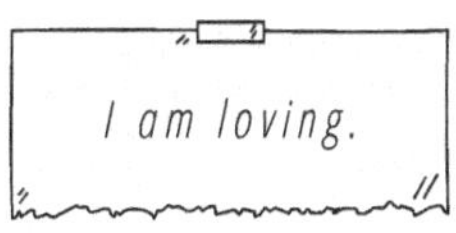

My Itinerary

6AM	
7AM	
8AM	
9AM	
10AM	
11AM	
12PM	
1PM	
2PM	
3PM	
4PM	
5PM	
6PM	
7PM	
8PM	
9PM	
10PM	

Notes

3 things I'm grateful for

○

○

○

My intentions

○

○

○

○

My priorities

○

○

○

○

Personal Check-in

How Am I Doing?	What Do I Need?	What Can I Start?

New Contacts

Name	Phone	Email	Follow Up Note

Celebrate Wins

People Served	Breakthrough Moments

To Do Items

Reflections

What Went Well	Lessons Learned	Apologies I Should Make

Who Should I Forgive	Points of Clarity	3 Things I'm Grateful For

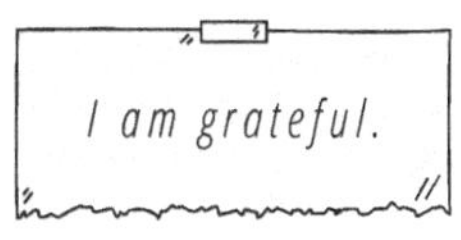

My Itinerary

6AM	
7AM	
8AM	
9AM	
10AM	
11AM	
12PM	
1PM	
2PM	
3PM	
4PM	
5PM	
6PM	
7PM	
8PM	
9PM	
10PM	

Notes

3 things I'm grateful for

My intentions

My priorities

Personal Check-in

How Am I Doing?

What Do I Need?

What Can I Start?

New Contacts

Name	Phone	Email	Follow Up Note

Celebrate Wins

People Served	Breakthrough Moments

To Do Items

Reflections

What Went Well

Lessons Learned

Apologies I Should Make

Who Should I Forgive

Points of Clarity

3 Things I'm Grateful For

Jan   Feb   Mar   Apr   May   Jun   Jul   Aug   Sep   Oct   Nov   Dec
1 2 3 4 5 6 7 8 9 10 11 12 13 14 15 16 17 18 19 20 21 22 23 24 25 26 27 28 29 30 31
Sunday   Monday   Tuesday   Wednesday   Thursday   Friday   Saturday

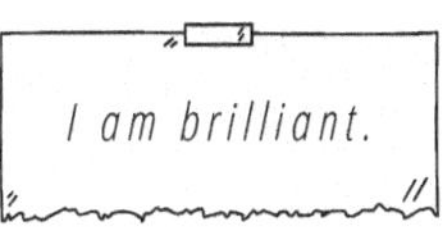

My Itinerary

6AM	
7AM	
8AM	
9AM	
10AM	
11AM	
12PM	
1PM	
2PM	
3PM	
4PM	
5PM	
6PM	
7PM	
8PM	
9PM	
10PM	

Notes

3 things I'm grateful for

○

○

○

My intentions

○

○

○

○

My priorities

○

○

○

○

Personal Check-in

How Am I Doing?	What Do I Need?	What Can I Start?

New Contacts

Name	Phone	Email	Follow Up Note

Celebrate Wins

People Served	Breakthrough Moments

To Do Items

Reflections

What Went Well	Lessons Learned	Apologies I Should Make

Who Should I Forgive	Points of Clarity	3 Things I'm Grateful For

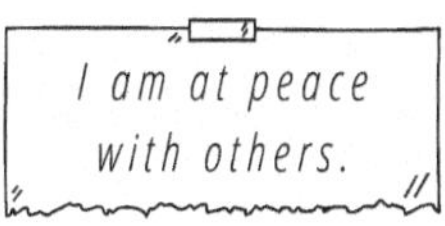

My Itinerary

6AM	
7AM	
8AM	
9AM	
10AM	
11AM	
12PM	
1PM	
2PM	
3PM	
4PM	
5PM	
6PM	
7PM	
8PM	
9PM	
10PM	

3 things I'm grateful for

○

○

○

My intentions

○

○

○

○

My priorities

○

○

○

○

Notes

Personal Check-in

How Am I Doing?

What Do I Need?

What Can I Start?

New Contacts

Name	Phone	Email	Follow Up Note

Celebrate Wins

To Do Items

People Served	Breakthrough Moments

Reflections

What Went Well

Lessons Learned

Apologies I Should Make

Who Should I Forgive

Points of Clarity

3 Things I'm Grateful For

Jan   Feb   Mar   Apr   May   Jun   Jul   Aug   Sep   Oct   Nov   Dec
1 2 3 4 5 6 7 8 9 10 11 12 13 14 15 16 17 18 19 20 21 22 23 24 25 26 27 28 29 30 31
Sunday   Monday   Tuesday   Wednesday   Thursday   Friday   Saturday

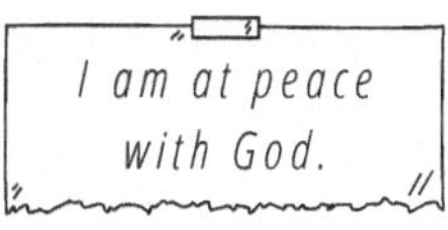

My Itinerary

6AM	
7AM	
8AM	
9AM	
10AM	
11AM	
12PM	
1PM	
2PM	
3PM	
4PM	
5PM	
6PM	
7PM	
8PM	
9PM	
10PM	

Notes

3 things I'm grateful for

○

○

○

My intentions

○

○

○

○

My priorities

○

○

○

○

Personal Check-in

How Am I Doing?	What Do I Need?	What Can I Start?

New Contacts

Name	Phone	Email	Follow Up Note

Celebrate Wins

People Served	Breakthrough Moments

To Do Items

Reflections

What Went Well	Lessons Learned	Apologies I Should Make

Who Should I Forgive	Points of Clarity	3 Things I'm Grateful For

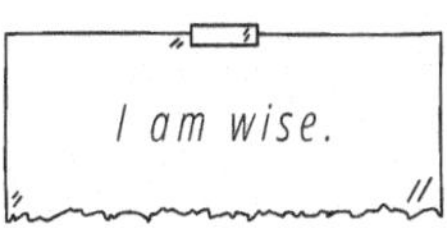

My Itinerary

6AM	
7AM	
8AM	
9AM	
10AM	
11AM	
12PM	
1PM	
2PM	
3PM	
4PM	
5PM	
6PM	
7PM	
8PM	
9PM	
10PM	

Notes

3 things I'm grateful for

- ○
- ○
- ○

My intentions

- ○
- ○
- ○
- ○

My priorities

- ○
- ○
- ○
- ○

Personal Check-in

How Am I Doing?	What Do I Need?	What Can I Start?

New Contacts

Name	Phone	Email	Follow Up Note

Celebrate Wins

People Served	Breakthrough Moments

To Do Items

Reflections

What Went Well	Lessons Learned	Apologies I Should Make

Who Should I Forgive	Points of Clarity	3 Things I'm Grateful For

Jan Feb Mar Apr May Jun Jul Aug Sep Oct Nov Dec
1 2 3 4 5 6 7 8 9 10 11 12 13 14 15 16 17 18 19 20 21 22 23 24 25 26 27 28 29 30 31
Sunday Monday Tuesday Wednesday Thursday Friday Saturday

My Itinerary

6AM	
7AM	
8AM	
9AM	
10AM	
11AM	
12PM	
1PM	
2PM	
3PM	
4PM	
5PM	
6PM	
7PM	
8PM	
9PM	
10PM	

Notes

3 things I'm grateful for

○

○

○

My intentions

○

○

○

○

My priorities

○

○

○

○

Personal Check-in

How Am I Doing?	What Do I Need?	What Can I Start?

New Contacts

Name	Phone	Email	Follow Up Note

Celebrate Wins

People Served	Breakthrough Moments

To Do Items

Reflections

What Went Well	Lessons Learned	Apologies I Should Make

Who Should I Forgive	Points of Clarity	3 Things I'm Grateful For

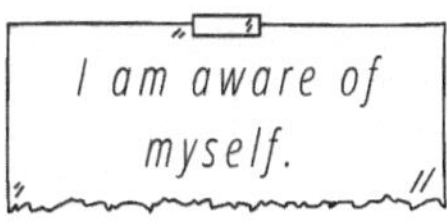

My Itinerary

6AM	
7AM	
8AM	
9AM	
10AM	
11AM	
12PM	
1PM	
2PM	
3PM	
4PM	
5PM	
6PM	
7PM	
8PM	
9PM	
10PM	

Notes

3 things I'm grateful for

○

○

○

My intentions

○

○

○

○

My priorities

○

○

○

○

Personal Check-in

How Am I Doing?	What Do I Need?	What Can I Start?

New Contacts

Name	Phone	Email	Follow Up Note

Celebrate Wins

To Do Items

People Served	Breakthrough Moments

Reflections

What Went Well	Lessons Learned	Apologies I Should Make

Who Should I Forgive	Points of Clarity	3 Things I'm Grateful For

Jan   Feb   Mar   Apr   May   Jun   Jul   Aug   Sep   Oct   Nov   Dec
1 2 3 4 5 6 7 8 9 10 11 12 13 14 15 16 17 18 19 20 21 22 23 24 25 26 27 28 29 30 31
Sunday   Monday   Tuesday   Wednesday   Thursday   Friday   Saturday

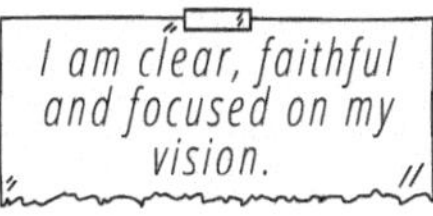

My Itinerary

6 AM	
7 AM	
8 AM	
9 AM	
10 AM	
11 AM	
12 PM	
1 PM	
2 PM	
3 PM	
4 PM	
5 PM	
6 PM	
7 PM	
8 PM	
9 PM	
10 PM	

Notes

3 things I'm grateful for

○

○

○

My intentions

○

○

○

○

My priorities

○

○

○

○

Personal Check-in

How Am I Doing?	What Do I Need?	What Can I Start?

New Contacts

Name	Phone	Email	Follow Up Note

Celebrate Wins

People Served	Breakthrough Moments

To Do Items

Reflections

What Went Well	Lessons Learned	Apologies I Should Make

Who Should I Forgive	Points of Clarity	3 Things I'm Grateful For

Jan   Feb   Mar   Apr   May   Jun   Jul   Aug   Sep   Oct   Nov   Dec
1 2 3 4 5 6 7 8 9 10 11 12 13 14 15 16 17 18 19 20 21 22 23 24 25 26 27 28 29 30 31
Sunday   Monday   Tuesday   Wednesday   Thursday   Friday   Saturday

My Itinerary

6AM	
7AM	
8AM	
9AM	
10AM	
11AM	
12PM	
1PM	
2PM	
3PM	
4PM	
5PM	
6PM	
7PM	
8PM	
9PM	
10PM	

Notes

3 things I'm grateful for

My intentions

My priorities

Personal Check-in

How Am I Doing?

What Do I Need?

What Can I Start?

New Contacts

Name	Phone	Email	Follow Up Note

Celebrate Wins

People Served

Breakthrough Moments

To Do Items

Reflections

What Went Well

Lessons Learned

Apologies I Should Make

Who Should I Forgive

Points of Clarity

3 Things I'm Grateful For

Jan   Feb   Mar   Apr   May   Jun   Jul   Aug   Sep   Oct   Nov   Dec
1 2 3 4 5 6 7 8 9 10 11 12 13 14 15 16 17 18 19 20 21 22 23 24 25 26 27 28 29 30 31
Sunday   Monday   Tuesday   Wednesday   Thursday   Friday   Saturday

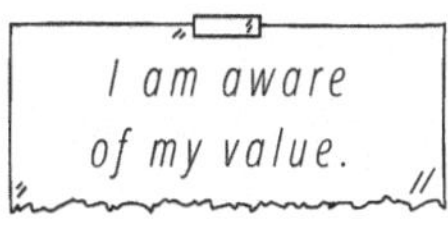

My Itinerary

6AM	
7AM	
8AM	
9AM	
10AM	
11AM	
12PM	
1PM	
2PM	
3PM	
4PM	
5PM	
6PM	
7PM	
8PM	
9PM	
10PM	

Notes

3 things I'm grateful for

○

○

○

My intentions

○

○

○

○

My priorities

○

○

○

○

Personal Check-in

How Am I Doing?	What Do I Need?	What Can I Start?

New Contacts

Name	Phone	Email	Follow Up Note

Celebrate Wins

People Served	Breakthrough Moments

To Do Items

Reflections

What Went Well	Lessons Learned	Apologies I Should Make

Who Should I Forgive	Points of Clarity	3 Things I'm Grateful For

Jan   Feb   Mar   Apr   May   Jun   Jul   Aug   Sep   Oct   Nov   Dec
1 2 3 4 5 6 7 8 9 10 11 12 13 14 15 16 17 18 19 20 21 22 23 24 25 26 27 28 29 30 31
Sunday   Monday   Tuesday   Wednesday   Thursday   Friday   Saturday

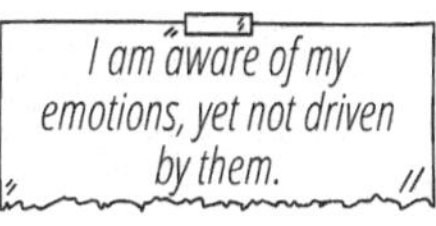

My Itinerary

6AM	
7AM	
8AM	
9AM	
10AM	
11AM	
12PM	
1PM	
2PM	
3PM	
4PM	
5PM	
6PM	
7PM	
8PM	
9PM	
10PM	

Notes

3 things I'm grateful for

○

○

○

My intentions

○

○

○

○

My priorities

○

○

○

○

Personal Check-in

How Am I Doing?

What Do I Need?

What Can I Start?

New Contacts

Name	Phone	Email	Follow Up Note

Celebrate Wins

People Served	Breakthrough Moments

To Do Items

Reflections

What Went Well

Lessons Learned

Apologies I Should Make

Who Should I Forgive

Points of Clarity

3 Things I'm Grateful For

Jan   Feb   Mar   Apr   May   Jun   Jul   Aug   Sep   Oct   Nov   Dec
1 2 3 4 5 6 7 8 9 10 11 12 13 14 15 16 17 18 19 20 21 22 23 24 25 26 27 28 29 30 31
Sunday   Monday   Tuesday   Wednesday   Thursday   Friday   Saturday

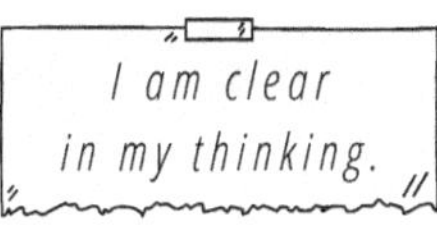

My Itinerary

6AM	
7AM	
8AM	
9AM	
10AM	
11AM	
12PM	
1PM	
2PM	
3PM	
4PM	
5PM	
6PM	
7PM	
8PM	
9PM	
10PM	

Notes

3 things I'm grateful for

- ○
- ○
- ○

My intentions

- ○
- ○
- ○
- ○

My priorities

- ○
- ○
- ○
- ○

Personal Check-in

How Am I Doing?	What Do I Need?	What Can I Start?

New Contacts

Name	Phone	Email	Follow Up Note

Celebrate Wins

People Served	Breakthrough Moments

To Do Items

Reflections

What Went Well	Lessons Learned	Apologies I Should Make

Who Should I Forgive	Points of Clarity	3 Things I'm Grateful For

My Itinerary

6AM	
7AM	
8AM	
9AM	
10AM	
11AM	
12PM	
1PM	
2PM	
3PM	
4PM	
5PM	
6PM	
7PM	
8PM	
9PM	
10PM	

Notes

3 things I'm grateful for

○

○

○

My intentions

○

○

○

○

My priorities

○

○

○

○

Personal Check-in

How Am I Doing? | What Do I Need? | What Can I Start?

New Contacts

Name | Phone | Email | Follow Up Note

Celebrate Wins

To Do Items

People Served | Breakthrough Moments

Reflections

What Went Well | Lessons Learned | Apologies I Should Make

Who Should I Forgive | Points of Clarity | 3 Things I'm Grateful For

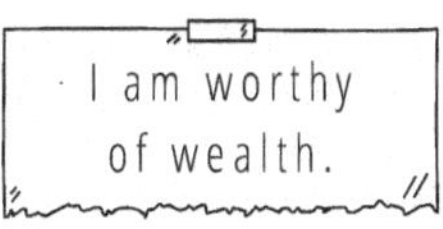

My Itinerary

6AM	
7AM	
8AM	
9AM	
10AM	
11AM	
12PM	
1PM	
2PM	
3PM	
4PM	
5PM	
6PM	
7PM	
8PM	
9PM	
10PM	

Notes

3 things I'm grateful for

○

○

○

My intentions

○

○

○

○

My priorities

○

○

○

○

Personal Check-in

How Am I Doing?	What Do I Need?	What Can I Start?

New Contacts

Name	Phone	Email	Follow Up Note

Celebrate Wins

People Served	Breakthrough Moments

To Do Items

Reflections

What Went Well	Lessons Learned	Apologies I Should Make

Who Should I Forgive	Points of Clarity	3 Things I'm Grateful For

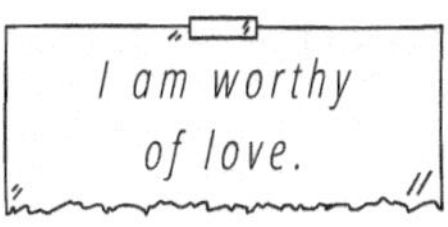

My Itinerary

6AM	
7AM	
8AM	
9AM	
10AM	
11AM	
12PM	
1PM	
2PM	
3PM	
4PM	
5PM	
6PM	
7PM	
8PM	
9PM	
10PM	

Notes

3 things I'm grateful for

○

○

○

My intentions

○

○

○

○

My priorities

○

○

○

○

Personal Check-in

How Am I Doing?	What Do I Need?	What Can I Start?

New Contacts

Name	Phone	Email	Follow Up Note

Celebrate Wins

People Served	Breakthrough Moments

To Do Items

Reflections

What Went Well	Lessons Learned	Apologies I Should Make

Who Should I Forgive	Points of Clarity	3 Things I'm Grateful For

NOTES

NOTES

NOTES

NOTES